Engaging God's Word

Galatians

Engage Bible Studies
Tools That Transform

Engage Bible Studies

an imprint of

 COMMUNITY BIBLE STUDY

Engaging God's Word: Galatians
Copyright © 2012, 2014 by Community Bible Study. All rights reserved.
ISBN 978-1-62194-001-2

Published by Community Bible Study
790 Stout Road
Colorado Springs, CO 80921-3802
1-800-826-4181
www.communitybiblestudy.org

Printed in the United States of America.

Contents

Introduction

Welcome to the life-changing adventure of engaging with God's Word! Whether this is the first time you've opened a Bible or you've studied the Scriptures all your life, good things are in store for you. Studying the Bible is unlike any other kind of study you have ever done. That's because the Word of God is *"living and active"* (Hebrews 4:12) and transcends time and cultures. The earth and heavens as we know them will one day pass away, but God's Word never will (Mark 13:31). It's as relevant to your life today as it was to the people who wrote it down centuries ago. And the fact that God's Word is living and active means that reading God's Word is always meant to be a personal experience. God's Word is not just dead words on a page—it is page after page of living, powerful words—so get ready, because the time you spend studying the Bible in this *Engaging God's Word* course will be life-transforming!

Why Study the Bible?

Some Christians read the Bible because they know they're supposed to. It's a good thing to do, and God expects it. And all that's true! However, there are many additional reasons to study God's Word. Here are just some of them.

We get to know God through His Word. Our God is a relational God who knows us and wants us to know Him. The Scriptures, which He authored, reveal much about Him: how He thinks and feels, what His purposes are, what He thinks about us, how He views the world He made, what He has planned for the future. The Bible shows us God's many attributes—His kindness, goodness, justice, love, faithfulness, mercy, compassion, creativity, redemption, sovereignty, and so on. As we get to know Him through His Word, we come to love and trust Him.

God speaks to us through His Word. One of the primary ways God speaks to us is through His written Word. Don't be surprised if, as you read the Bible, certain parts nearly jump off the page at you, almost as if they'd been written with you in mind. God is the Author of this incredible book, so that's not just possible, it's likely! Whether it is to find comfort, warning, correction, teaching, or guidance, always approach God's Word with your spiritual ears open (Isaiah 55:3) because God, your loving heavenly Father, has things He wants to say to you.

God's Word brings life. Just about everyone wants to learn the secret to "the good life." And the good news is, that secret is found in God's Word. Don't think of the Bible as a bunch of rules. Viewing it with that mindset is a distortion. God gave us His Word because as our Creator and the Creator of the universe, He alone knows how life was meant to work. He knows that love makes us happier than hate, that generosity brings more joy than greed, and that integrity allows us to rest more peacefully at night than deception does. God's ways are not always "easiest" but they are the way to life. As the Psalmist says, *"If Your law had not been my delight, I would have perished in my affliction. I will never forget Your precepts, for by them You have given me life"* (Psalm 119:92-93).

God's Word offers stability in an unstable world. Truth is an ever-changing negotiable for many people in our culture today. But building your life on constantly changing "truth" is like building your house on shifting sand. God's Word, like God Himself, never changes. What He says was true yesterday, is true today, and will still be true a billion years from now. Jesus said, *"Everyone then who hears these words of Mine and does them will be like a wise man who built his house on the rock"* (Matthew 7:24).

God's Word helps us to pray effectively. When we read God's Word and get to know what He is really like, we understand better how to pray. God answers prayers that are according to His will. We discover His will by reading the Bible. First John 5:14-15 tells us that *"this is the confidence that we have toward Him, that if we ask anything according to His will He hears us. And if we know that He hears us in whatever we ask, we know that we have the requests that we have asked of Him."*

How to Get the Most out of *Engaging God's Word*

Each *Engaging God's Word* study contains key elements that have been carefully designed to help you get the most out of your time in God's Word. Slightly modified for your study-at-home success, this approach is very similar to the tried-and-proven Bible study method that Community Bible Study has used with thousands of men, women, and children across the United States and around the world for nearly 40 years. There are some basic things you can expect to find in each course in this series.

❖ Lesson 1 provides an overview of the Bible book (or books) you will study and questions to help you focus, anticipate, and pray about what you will be learning.

❖ Every lesson contains questions to answer on your own, commentary that reviews and clarifies the passage, and three special sections called "Apply what you have learned," "Think about" and "Personalize this lesson."

❖ Some lessons contain memory verse suggestions.

Whether you plan to use *Engaging God's Word* on your own or with a group, here are some suggestions that will help you enjoy and receive the most benefit from your study.

Spread out each lesson over several days. Your *Engaging God's Word* lessons were designed to take a week to complete. Spreading out your study rather than doing it all at once allows time for the things God is teaching you to sink in and for you to practice applying them.

Pray each time you read God's Word. The Bible is a book unlike any other because God Himself inspired it. The same Spirit who inspired the human authors who wrote it will help you to understand and apply it if you ask Him to. So make it a practice to ask Him to make His Word come alive to you every time you read it.

Read the whole passage covered in the lesson. Before plunging into the questions, take time to read the specific chapter or verses that will be covered in that lesson. Doing this will give you important context for the whole lesson. Reading the Bible in context is an important principle in interpreting it accurately.

Begin learning the memory verse. Learning Scripture by heart requires discipline, but the rewards far outweigh the effort. Memorizing a verse allows you to recall it whenever you need it—for personal encouragement and direction, or to share with someone else. Consider writing the verse on a sticky note or index card that you can post where you will see it often or carry with you to review during the day. Reading and re-reading the verse often—out loud when possible—is a simple way to commit it to memory.

Re-read the passage for each section of questions. Each lesson is divided into sections so that you study one small part of Scripture at a time. Before attempting to answer the questions, review the verses that the questions will cover.

Answer the questions without consulting the Commentary or other reference materials. There is great joy in having the Holy Spirit teach you God's Word on your own, without the help of outside resources. Don't cheat yourself of the delight of discovery by reading the Commentary prematurely. Wait until after you've completed the lesson.

Repeat the process for all the question sections.

Prayerfully consider the "Apply what you have learned," marked with the ✒ push pin symbol. The vision of Community Bible Study is not to just gain knowledge about the Bible, but to be transformed by it. For this reason, each set of questions closes with a section that encourages you to apply what you are learning. Usually this section involves action—something for you to do. As you practice these suggestions, your life will change.

Read the Commentary. *Engaging God's Word* commentaries are written by theologians whose goal is to help you understand the context of what you are studying as it relates to the rest of Scripture, God's character, and what the passage means for your life. Of necessity, the commentaries include the author's interpretations. While interesting and helpful, keep in mind that the Commentary is simply one person's understanding of what these passages mean. Other godly men and women have views that are also worth considering.

Pause to contemplate each "Think about" section, marked with the notepad symbol. These features, embedded in the Commentary, offer a place to pause and consider some of the principles being brought out by the text. They provide excellent ideas to journal about or to discuss with other believers, especially those doing the study with you.

Jot down insights or prayer points from the "Personalize this lesson" marked with the ☑ check box symbol. While the "Apply what you have learned" section focuses on doing, the "Personalize this lesson" section focuses on becoming. Spiritual transformation is not just about doing right things and refraining from doing wrong things—it is about changing from the inside out. To be transformed means letting God change our hearts so that our attitudes, emotions, desires, reactions, and goals are increasingly like Jesus'. Often this section will discuss something that you cannot do in your own strength—so your response will usually be something to pray about. Remember that becoming more Christ-like is not just a matter of trying harder—it requires God's empowerment.

Cherish Your Freedom in Christ
Galatians 1:1-10

In the world the apostle Paul inhabited people were clearly defined as either Jews or Gentiles. Jews had God's laws, and most Jews were proud of their pious efforts to obey them. Most Gentiles were ignorant of God's laws, made no effort to obey them, and were immoral. Not surprisingly, then, because the first members of the church were Jews, the first controversy the church faced was not immorality but legalism. When Gentiles began to join the church, "Judaizers" wanted these Gentiles to follow the Jewish laws. The church in Galatia was made up primarily of Gentiles, and the Judaizers arguments were beginning to sway them. Immorality is a problem, but legalism is not the solution. Paul had to intervene. In this letter we will see Paul make several points as he pleads with the Galatians to resist legalism and live by faith.

❖ He defends his God-given authority.

❖ He defends his call to take the gospel to the Gentiles.

❖ He defends the principle of justification by faith.

❖ He cites the Torah (the Old Testament) as upholding the principle of justification by faith.

❖ He cites the Holy Spirit as the power to enable believers to live righteously by faith.

❖ He cites the need for believers to help one another to live righteously by faith.

1. Have you, or anyone you know, struggled with trying to please God through your own efforts?

   _____

   _____

   _____

   _____

2. Are you surprised to hear that the Old Testament upholds the principle of justification by faith? Why might this thought surprise some people?

   _____

   _____

   _____

3. What questions arise as you contemplate the Holy Spirit empowering you to live by faith?

   _____

   _____

   _____

   _____

Take a few minutes to list areas in your life in which your actions might be motivated more by legalism or fear than by the Holy Spirit. If you are studying with a group, share those thoughts with the group members. Then, at the conclusion of the six-lesson study, look back at the list and see how your motivations are changing.

Lesson 1

Cherish Your Freedom in Christ
Galatians 1:1-10

Few books have had a more profound influence on the history of the Christian world than the apostle Paul's letter to the Galatians. Composed almost 2,000 years ago, Galatians' six short chapters address two important doctrines—justification by faith and freedom from the Law. It is a "Declaration of Independence" from legalism.

On Paul's first missionary journey (Acts 13–14), he founded churches in southern Galatia (central Turkey). On the second trip, he brought them a letter from the Jerusalem Council and confirmed them in the faith (Acts 15:1-16:5). Because Paul writes nothing of his imprisonment in the letter, he was probably still free to travel when he wrote. This would set the date of writing after AD 47, when he first journeyed through Galatia, and before AD 58, when he was arrested.

A New Emphasis

In Paul's time, the new church was grappling with radical changes, and Jewish Christians were rethinking their identity. Jesus and His disciples were Jews; therefore, after Christ's crucifixion and resurrection, the apostles, Jews who became the leaders of the early Christians, still saw the Mosaic Law as binding. Their belief that Jesus was the long-awaited Messiah was hard to reconcile with the traditional view of an exalted Messiah, especially because Jesus had been nailed to a cross, like a common criminal. The Resurrection, however, revived the hope of these followers that, as Old Testament taught, the Messiah would return in power to establish His kingdom.

The apostles invited all Jews to share in the gift of salvation through faith in their resurrected Messiah and then receive the Holy Spirit (Acts 2:37-38). Eventually they would participate in the day of Christ's return (Acts 3:19-21). The book of Acts tells how the church came to understand that they needed to communicate the gospel in terms that would appeal not only to orthodox Jews, but also to Gentiles, who knew little about the Mosaic Law.

Should Gentiles Be Included?

As persecuted Christians were driven from Jerusalem, the gospel was planted in the surrounding region. Many Gentiles wanted to be admitted into the church. The gospel message was one of reconciliation: of God with humanity, and of people with other people by breaking down barriers between races, classes, and sexes. The church had to consider whether full membership should be reserved only for Jews and those who were willing to become Jews by accepting all the requirements of Old Testament Law, including circumcision. Should status be given to Gentiles who acknowledged Jesus Christ as Lord, but were unwilling to become Jews to enter His church? Church leaders addressed these questions at the Jerusalem Council. Their decision allowed Gentiles into fellowship without burdening them with following all the Mosaic Law's rituals.

Greeting (Galatians 1:1-5)

The letter's opening reveals that Paul is greatly disturbed by news he has received concerning the Galatian church. Without his usual greeting, he plunges into the problem at hand. A group known as Judaizers has challenged Paul's authority as an apostle. These Jews accept the gospel, but claim that no Gentile can be a Christian without first becoming a Jew by submitting to Jewish rites. Paul moves quickly to refute the Judaizers' claim that he was not a true apostle. The Greek word translated *apostle* means *one sent forth*. While it was technically applied to the Twelve who had been with Christ (Acts 1:21-26), the word also denotes a special authority in spiritual matters. Men like Barnabas, who traveled with Paul on the first missionary journey, were also called apostles in this more general sense. The apostles became pioneers in taking the gospel to new territories and planting churches there.

The phrase *"the churches of Galatia"* (Galatians 1:2) indicates that the letter was circulated among several churches, probably in Pisidian Antioch, Iconium, Lystra, Derbe, and others in the province. Galatians 1:4-5 defines the letter's central doctrinal issue and pinpoints the controversy. Paul declares what the Lord has done: Christ *"gave Himself for our sins to deliver us from the present evil age."*

A Threat to Truth (Galatians 1:6-10)

Convinced that the gospel is at stake, Paul speaks bluntly about the changes occurring in the Galatian churches. He is astonished that so soon after their conversion some believers are turning to false teachers who seek to transfer loyalty from Christ to the Mosaic Law.

Gospel means *good news*. The good news is that God through Christ has provided salvation to all who believe. Such a redeeming work is available by God's working, not by trying to conform to the Law. The Judaizers' claim their teaching to be another gospel, but it is not good news at all. If salvation depends on what one does, our hope is crushed. Paul pronounces a curse on anyone who dares to pervert the gospel. His reference to *"an angel from heaven"* (1:8) may acknowledge Satan's ability to masquerade *"as an angel of light"* (2 Corinthians 11:14), or may emphasize the point that no one, including a divine messenger, has the authority to change the truth of the gospel.

Think about how Paul was flexible on non-essentials such as whether one ate meat or only vegetables. However, he was not dealing with petty disagreements, but about the very truth of salvation. When you believe in Jesus Christ as Savior and Lord, you must reject anything that contradicts or modifies the all-sufficiency of His work on the Cross. Jesus said following Him involved a choice, comparing it to a *"narrow gate"* (Matthew 7:13-14). The gospel is no longer "good news" if it loses its message of salvation by grace alone.

Apostleship Questioned

Apparently Paul faced allegations that he had watered down the Law's rigorous requirements to gain the Gentiles' approval. On the contrary, his refusal to compromise and his strong condemnation of the false teachers proves that Paul seeks divine approval, not the approval of people.

Personalize this lesson.

✓ Paul moved quickly and firmly to counter the false doctrine being spread through Galatia and reestablish the truth. The severity of his words grew out of his love for the Galatians. These young churches survived and grew larger and stronger, at least in part because Paul told them what they needed to hear, not just what they wanted to hear. Do we have the courage and conviction to correct error and confront sin as Paul did? We need to ask for the Holy Spirit's guidance so that we respond in a way that honors God. Paul's actions serve as a good example for us. He confronted the believers in love and wished them *"grace to you and peace"* (1:3). He was a *"servant of Christ"* (1:10), seeking to please His Savior and uncompromising when the truth of the gospel was at stake. We are told to *"let the word of Christ dwell in you richly, teaching and admonishing one another in all wisdom"* (Colossians 3:16).

Paul Establishes His Apostolic Authority
Galatians 1:11-2:21

Memorize God's Word: Galatians 2:20.

❖ Galatians 1:1-17—God Calls Paul

1. Who is the author of the gospel Paul preaches?

   _____

   _____

2. Read 1:6-9. Do you think some Christians today are still being confused and deceived by *"a gospel contrary to the one we preached to you"*?

   _____

   _____

   _____

3. What results might you expect to come from following *"a different gospel"*?

   _____

   _____

   _____

4. In 1:13-14, when Paul speaks of *"my former life,"* how does he describe it?

   _____

   _____

5. What is Paul's specific calling (Galatians 1:16-17; Acts 26:15-18)?

_____

_____

❖ Galatians 1:18-24—Paul Visits Jerusalem

6. Why do you think Paul wants to meet Peter? (See Acts 11:1-18.)

_____

_____

7. What is the main point of Galatians 1:24?

_____

_____

8. Have you ever praised God for the positive changes you have seen in the life of a fellow Christian? Give an example.

_____

_____

_____

_____

❖ Galatians 2:1-10—The Apostles Accept Paul

9. Why did Paul return to Jerusalem?

_____

_____

10. What motivates Paul's strong stand (2:4-5)?

_____

_____

11. How does our culture today threaten to restrict *"the truth of the gospel"*?

_____

_____

12. What is Paul's attitude toward the leaders of the Jerusalem church? (See also 1 Corinthians 1:26-31; James 4:6.)

_____

_____

13. What does *"the right hand of fellowship"* signify?

_____

_____

14. How does 2:10 show us that the *"fellowship"* of Christians goes beyond agreement on doctrinal issues? (See also 1 John 3:16-18.)

_____

_____

❖ Galatians 2:11-14—Paul Confronts Peter

15. Describe Peter's behavior before and after the group sent by James comes to Antioch.

_____

_____

16. What do you think Paul expects of people who are *"in step with the truth of the gospel"* (Galatians 2:14; see also 3:26-29)?

_____

_____

_____

❖ Galatians 2:15-21—A Resolute Stand

17. Justification means that God has pardoned those who believe in Christ from the penalty of sin. What does *"justified by faith in Christ"* (2:16) mean to you? (See also Ephesians 2:8-9.)

_____

_____

_____

18. Why do you think living for God requires that we die to the Law (Galatians 2:19; see also Romans 8:1-4)?

_____

_____

_____

19. What does Galatians 2:20 mean to you?

_____

_____

_____

20. In 2:21, *"grace"* and *"law"* are declared to be incompatible as far as salvation is concerned. How do you explain the tendency of people to revert, as Peter did, to "law-keeping"?

_____

_____

_____

_____

Apply what you have learned. For Paul, Christ's death meant everything: *"I do not treat the grace of God as meaningless. For if keeping the law could make us right with God, then there was no need for Christ to die"* (Galatians 2:21, NLT). Our efforts to be righteous are useless. By grace, God accepts Jesus' death as payment for our sins. Are you, like Paul, able to say that your life has meaning because of what Christ has done for you?

Paul Establishes His Apostolic Authority
Galatians 1:11-2:21

Paul's Conversion and Call (Galatians 1:11-17)

Paul's opening statements present a response to the Judaizers' attack on his authority and message. Paul states that, by direct revelation, Jesus Christ transmitted the gospel to him and equipped him to preach. He reviews the amazing event on the Damascus road (Acts 9). Paul points out the extremes of his former position and the great gulf between it and the position he now holds; divine, supernatural intervention completely turned his life around.

Think about how the dramatic change in Paul's life demonstrates God's power and grace. Every conversion comes by God's grace and power. When a "nice" sinner believes in Christ, it is no less a miracle than that of an obvious sinner, even if it is less dramatic. Human nature, apart from the work of the Holy Spirit, cannot understand or believe the gospel. Whether you came to know the Lord later in life or were nurtured by Christian parents so that you cannot remember a time when you did not know Christ as your Lord, the Holy Spirit was the agent of conversion.

Paul's First Visit to Jerusalem (Galatians 1:18-24)

Paul's purpose for visiting Jerusalem was personal—*"to visit Cephas* [Peter]*"* (1:18). He spent 15 days with Peter, leader of the original 12 apostles. Possibly motivated by the Judaizers' insinuations that his visit

to Jerusalem was unimportant, Paul assures the churches that he is not lying. He then spent time in Syria and Cilicia. The churches in Judea had only heard about the man who had formerly sought to wipe them out, but who now was proclaiming the gospel. Instead of belittling his work as the Judaizers were doing, those churches thanked God for what had happened in and through him.

Paul Returns to Jerusalem (Galatians 2:1-10)

"After fourteen years" (2:1), Paul officially confronts the church leaders in Jerusalem to defend the gospel against the intrusion of Jewish law. Accompanied by Barnabas and Titus, Paul met *"privately"* with the leaders, whose authority and standing within the Christian community he respected. Paul knew the success of his ministry did not depend on the verdict of these men, but his statement in 2:2, *"to make sure I was not running or had not run in vain"* implies that he understood the importance of maintaining the unity of the gospel. If other apostles did not agree with his stand on justification by faith without the works of the Law, Paul's mission to the Gentiles would be seriously weakened. His ministry efforts would be *"in vain"* if a division developed among the apostles, or if they rejected Paul's insistence that there must be only one unified church, open to Jews and Gentiles alike.

Far from challenging Paul's interpretation of the gospel, the apostles affirmed it. They even accepted Titus, an uncircumcised Gentile, despite objections from those who wanted all Christians to submit to circumcision. To Paul, circumcision had no bearing on one's salvation. The leaders in Jerusalem recognized that Paul had been called to a work among the Gentiles just as Peter had been called to the Jews. Peter, James, and John accepted Barnabas and Paul as partners in a common task. Probably, giving *"the right hand of fellowship"* was done in public. The leaders added one request: *"remember the poor"* (2:10).

Paul Confronts Peter (Galatians 2:11-14)

During a visit to Antioch, Peter had associated freely with the Gentile Christians—even eating with them. When men *"from James"* (2:12) arrived, Peter began to separate himself from the Gentile Christians. His influence led Barnabas and other Jewish Christians to do likewise.

Paul saw the problem clearly and spoke out against Peter on the matter of principle. Because Peter acted in public, Paul faced him publicly. It appeared that Peter's refusal to eat with Gentile Christians and other Jewish members of the Antioch church left the Gentiles no choice but to conform to the Jewish dietary laws or suffer a division in the church.

Justification by Faith (Galatians 2:15-21)

Paul introduces his discourse on justification by faith by explaining that, although the Jews are privileged people, following the Law could never make them righteous in God's sight. Only by faith in Christ and His merits, not by works of the Law, could they receive this blessing. In 2:16, Paul introduces the term *justified*. To *justify* is used in a legal sense as a gracious act whereby God, because Christ has paid the penalty, declares *just* the sinner, who then accepts the benefit only by faith. The sinner's guilt is put onto Christ and righteousness is credited to the sinner.

Paul points out that, through the Law, he realized his own sinfulness (Romans 3:20). At the same time, he despairs that the Law could do nothing to secure God's verdict of righteousness. Giving up all hope in the Law, he died to it forever. In the same breath that Paul says he has *"died to the law,"* he states what that death accomplishes—*"that I might live to God"* (Galatians 2:19). It is a paradox. At the moment of death, life enters. Being alive to God means being restored to new life and being responsive to God's grace and to His people.

Christianity is more than observing legalistic forms; it is life. Close identification with Christ leads the believer into spiritual fellowship with Him. Paul can now say that he has died to the past and risen in newness of life: *"It is no longer I who live, but Christ who lives in me"* (2:20). This is the new birth. By faith, Christ fills Paul's heart, soul, and being. He is Paul's righteousness, making possible God's verdict of acquittal.

Paul affirms what he has said to this point: *"I do not treat the grace of God as meaningless. For if keeping the law could make us right with God, then there was no need for Christ to die"* (2:21, NLT). If conforming to the Law has any merit, then Christ died for nothing. If His death and sacrifice were unnecessary, then grace would be done away with. Either Christ's death is all, or it is nothing.

Personalize this lesson.

☑ Believers in the Galatian churches thought that they needed to add something to what Christ had done on the cross. Christians today, like the Galatians, are tempted to do the same thing. "Christ plus …" The plus may be anything—a good cause, a particular set of rules of behavior, a prescribed dress code, membership in a particular church. If we add anything to God's gift of salvation, we are repeating the same problem Paul fought in Galatia.

Lesson 3

Faith or Law?
Galatians 3:1-4:7

Memorize God's Word: Galatians 3:28.

❖ Galatians 3:1-5—Paul Asks Key Questions

1. What message has *"bewitched"* (3:1) the Galatians? (See also 2:4-5, 15-16, 20b-21.)

   _____

   _____

2. In your own words, explain the conflict of belief Paul addresses in each of the questions in 3:2-5.

   _____

   _____

   _____

3. In what ways does today's Christian community still struggle with the same sort of thinking that the Galatian church did?

   _____

   _____

   _____

❖ Galatians 3:6-9—Old Testament Grace

4. From the following verses, list some facts about Abraham:

   a. Genesis 12:1-5 _____

b.   Genesis 17:3-8, 11 _____

c.   Hebrews 11:11-12 _____

5. Explain why Paul (quoting Genesis 15:6) says that *"Abraham believed God, and it was counted to him as righteousness."* (See also Romans 4:1-5, 10-12.)

6. Why does Paul say *"it is those of faith who are the sons of Abraham"* (Galatians 3:7)?

❖ Galatians 3:10-14—Redeemed Through Christ

7. Paul introduces us to a new term in Galatians 3:14. Using a dictionary, or any other word source, define *redeemed*.

8. Justice and grace are not mutually exclusive. Explain how redemption satisfies the Law:

a.   Romans 8:3-4 _____

b.   1 Peter 1:18-19 _____

_____

_____

9. For what reason did God redeem you (Galatians 3:14)?

_____

_____

10. What does *"the promised Spirit"* (3:14) mean? (See also John 14:15-17, 26; 16:7-14.)

_____

_____

❖ Galatians 3:15-25—The Law's Purpose

11. Why is the use of the singular noun *"offspring"* in Galatians 3:16 highly significant?

_____

_____

12. Why do you think Paul mentions the number of years between the making of the covenant with Abraham and the giving of the Law (3:17)?

_____

_____

13. Paul states that Law does have purpose. What is that purpose (3:19, 24)? (See also Romans 3:20.)

_____

_____

❖ Galatians 3:26–4:7-Our Standing in Christ

14. Paul states, *"You are all sons"* (3:26). Is there anything a person can do to earn this position (3:14, 26-29)? Explain your answer.

_____

_____

15. Compare having *"put on Christ"* to being clothed in garments you might wear any day. What is suggested by this symbolic language?

_____

_____

16. a. How were we, as believers, at one time like the child described in Galatians 4:1-3? _____

_____

_____

    b. How did our situation change? _____

_____

_____

17. What privileges or blessings of being *"an heir"* (4:7) give you joy?

_____

_____

Apply what you have learned. Paul challenged the Galatians to consider their identity in Christ. As Christians, being clothed with Christ frees us from human distinctions and enables us to see ourselves as God's children, no longer slaves but heirs with *"the full rights of sons"* (Galatians 4:5, NIV). God sends the Spirit of his Son into the heart of anyone who is His child (4:6). Are you enjoying a closeness with God that allows you to call Him *"Abba, Father"*?

Faith or Law?
Galatians 3:1-4:7

Paul Appeals to Experience (Galatians 3:1-5)

Paul's frustration is obvious as he defends the doctrine of justification. Addressing the churches as *"foolish Galatians!"* (3:1), he means they lack spiritual perception. Returning to the Law denies the sufficiency of Christ. Their irrational choice leads Paul to ask, *"Who has bewitched you?"* If their eyes had been fixed on Christ, they would not have been led astray so easily.

The Galatians understood that Jesus Christ was publicly crucified, yet they are about to turn from this truth as though it has no significance. To the early church, the Messiah's crucifixion, a violent and degrading death, was a recent and vivid image. But in 4:1, Paul appeals to more than historical fact; he wants them to grasp the eternal truth—Christ died in our place!

Through questions, Paul leads the Galatians to evaluate how God has been working in their lives. The Galatian church was essentially Gentile, with no covenant claim on God. They had received the Spirit through faith alone. The next question asks if they plan to perfect God's work through their own efforts: *"Surely you can't be so idiotic as to think that a man begins his spiritual life in the Spirit and then completes it by reverting to outward observances?"* (3:3, PH).

Paul recalls that God provided *"signs and wonders"* at Iconium (Acts 14:3) and cured a lame man at Lystra. Paul asks if they attribute these miracles of body and soul to observing the Law or to their faith in the living Christ (Galatians 3:5). Paul's questions would force them to examine their new life in Christ. They had moved abruptly from idol worship to the knowledge of a loving God. The contrast between the old and new life would be very great. Paul cries out for the Galatians to protect what has been freely given to them in love and sacrifice.

Paul Appeals to Scripture (Galatians 3:6-14)

To counter the Judaizers, Paul refers to God's promise that He would make Abraham the father of innumerable descendents. Abraham was justified by faith alone. Paul draws the conclusion: The Galatians and all believers are sons of Abraham through faith. Gentile believers are now counted as Abraham's offspring or spiritual sons. *"The Scripture foresaw that God would justify the Gentiles by faith"* (3:8, NIV), Paul states. God said directly to Abraham, *"In you all the families of the earth will be blessed"* (Genesis 12:3). As the prophesied Seed of Abraham, Christ is the Justifier, the Source of all blessing for all nations. Those who believe are *"blessed along with Abraham, the man of faith"* (Galatians 3:9).

Think about God called Abraham to settle in an unknown land and promised him countless descendants. Childless and old, Abraham continued to believe God. He was 100 years old when the promised son was born. His faith was counted to him as righteousness because he trusted God. Belief for its own sake is ineffective; the object of faith is what matters. Sometimes we rely on position, financial resources, medicine, and other people rather than leaning on God. While God does use those things for our benefit, they cannot provide salvation. When Christ is the object of faith, the blessings are eternal.

Paul divides people between those who depend on faith in God and those who depend on works of the Law. He announces that *"all who rely on works of the law are under a curse"* (3:10). They are under God's sovereign judgment and punishment. Paul uses Scripture to prove his point: *"Cursed be everyone who does not abide by all things written in the Book of the Law, and do them"* (Deuteronomy 27:26). One could escape condemnation by doing everything written in the Book of the Law—perfectly.

How, then, can one come into right relationship with God? Paul quotes an Old Testament prophet: *"The righteous shall live by his faith"* (Habakkuk 2:4). The Old and the New Testaments agree that a right relationship to God involves a personal act of trust in a Person rather than striving to conform to the Law's demands.

Paul Appeals to Reason (Galatians 3:15-25)

To explain the sanctity of the promise made to Abraham, Paul compares a confirmed, probated will to God's covenant. No valid will can be set aside for a substitute unless the document's originator initiates the change. God originated the Abrahamic covenant, and the promises were made to Abraham and his *seed*—singular. The specific heir referred to was Christ. From the beginning, God intended that the covenant of salvation would be fulfilled by a Savior, a Deliverer, not by following a set of laws. Being a physical descendant of Abraham is not enough to benefit from the inheritance; one must be a true believer. Because God initiated the promise to Abraham several hundred years before instituting the Law, the covenant is based on God's promise, not on observing the Law. The Galatians must decide whether they will choose human effort (observing the Law) or God's way (grace).

The Law's purpose is to expose sin. Paul rejects the idea that the Law contradicts the promises, for God gave both. If the Law had power to bestow life, then righteousness would come through keeping the Law. Instead, it reveals the world's imprisonment to sin and shows the need for salvation.

The Position of Sonship (Galatians 3:26-4:7)

Paul declares, *"In Christ Jesus you are all sons of God, through faith"* (3:26). Anyone who accepts Christ as Lord becomes one of God's sons, united to Christ, God's eternal Son. Society's distinctions are no longer important. During the time of the Mosaic Law, rigid differences were maintained between Jew and Gentile, free men and slaves, men and women. When Christ came, the distinctions were abolished.

A believer's sonship results in a close relationship with the Father. *Abba* is the Aramaic word that Jesus used in prayer; it is an affectionate term a Jewish child would use to address his or her father. All believers may call out *"Abba, Father"* to God with the confidence of one who knows a loving parent.

Personalize this lesson.

Because of God's grace, Christ fulfilled the Law's demands and paid the penalty of sin for us. Our freedom in Christ does not mean we may become lawbreakers, but we are free to live according to God's will. Paul offers the following counsel: *"Do not present your members to sin as instruments for unrighteousness… For sin will have no dominion over you, since you are not under law but under grace."* (Romans 6:12-14).

Children of Promise
Galatians 4:8-31

❖ **Galatians 4:8-16—A Plea Based on Friendship**

1. Why do you think Paul distinguishes between knowing God and being known by God (4:8-9)? (See also 1 Corinthians 8:3; 13:12; Psalm 139:1-6.)

    _____

    _____

    _____

2. What is Paul's main concern in Galatians 4:8-11?

    _____

    _____

    _____

3. Briefly describe the circumstances of their first meeting and the treatment Paul received from the Galatians (4:13-15).

    _____

    _____

    _____

4. What changes have occurred in the Galatians' attitude toward Paul and in their spiritual life?

    _____

    _____

5. What is the problem for Paul in 4:16?

    _____

    _____

6. How might telling a fellow Christians the truth cause problems
    in your relationships?

    _____

    _____

7. What can you learn from Paul's behavior and attitude about
    facing such situations?

    _____

    _____

❖ Galatians 4:17-20—Paul Warns the Galatians

8. What warnings does Paul give the Galatians about those who are
    disrupting their faith?

    _____

    _____

9. What is Paul implying about the Galatians in 4:18b?

    _____

    _____

10. What do you learn about Paul from 4:19-20 and
    1 Thessalonians 2:6-9?

    _____

    _____

    _____

❖ Galatians 4:21-28—Hagar and Sarah: An Illustration from Scripture

11. Paul uses Abraham's sons and their mothers to illustrate the
    difference between being enslaved by the Law and being free

in Christ. Read Genesis 16; 17:21; 21:1-7 and fill in the chart
below to help you understand the historical facts that form the
basis for the comparison.

	Sarah	Hagar
Status in Abraham's household:		
Son's name:		
Circumstances of son's birth:		
Covenant represented:		

12. Read Galatians 4:26 and Hebrews 12:18-24. From these
    passages, write the phrases that describe the heavenly Jerusalem.

    _____

    _____

    _____

❖ Galatians 4:29-31—Paul Concludes the Argument

13. From verse 29, describe the problem that exists between Isaac
    and Ishmael. (See also Genesis 21:9-13.)

    _____

    _____

14. How is the same problem occurring among the Galatians?

    _____

    _____

15. Remembering that Paul is speaking figuratively, what point do
    you think he wants the Galatians to understand by his statement
    in 4:30?

    _____

    _____

Apply what you have learned. Paul's conviction that Christians are born to freedom has been fully presented. Like the Galatians, we sometimes forget that *"we are not children of the slave but of the free woman"* (4:31). By faith in Christ, not human effort, we experience the freedom of living as one of God's children. Prayerfully examine your own life and ask God to help you get rid of anything that prevents you from your inheritance *"with the son of the free woman"* (4:30).

Children of Promise
Galatians 4:8-31

Paul Expresses Concern (Galatians 4:8-20)

Paul expresses shock that people who have experienced grace in Jesus Christ would turn back to principles that rely on human effort and understanding. The Galatians have turned to another system of bondage—the legalistic regulations of Jewish Law. But the Law was given to lead them to freedom in Christ. Law, like the *"weak and worthless elementary principles"* (4:9) of pagan religions, has no saving power.

Paul's words, *"Brothers, I entreat you"* (4:12) reveal his tenderness for the churches and the sense of urgency he feels because they are wandering from the truth. He wants the Galatians to experience the same full freedom from the Law that he has experienced. He begs them not to embrace the very Law he has given up, but to be as he is, free from all but Jesus Christ.

Think about leading through humility. Paul pleaded with the Galatians to *"become as I am."* Initially, such a plea might sound boastful, but Paul's plea was that the Galatians be like him in weakness. Some were tempting the Galatians to turn from the "weakness" of faith to the "strength" of works. But, as Paul wrote to the Corinthians, *"When I am weak, then I am strong"* (2 Corinthians 12:10). In what ways are you willing to follow Paul in being "weak" to the world's call to self-sufficiency?

After affirming their past relationship, Paul can proceed to more straight talk: *"What, then, has become of your blessedness?"* (4:15). Paul notes a change in their attitude. He asks if he is considered an enemy for telling them the truth and pointing out their real enemies, the Judaizers, who are trying to persuade the Galatians to adopt their teaching and reject the true gospel. Paul addresses the Galatians as *"my little children"* (4:19). He compares his concern to a mother giving birth. He had once endured labor pains for them until, by God's help, they trusted in Christ. Now, with false teachers alienating their affection, Paul's birth pangs have returned. His suffering will continue *"until Christ is formed in you"* (4:19). Paul wants his spiritual children to be like Christ in thought, aspiration, and will.

Allegory of Hagar and Sarah (Galatians 4:21-31)

With a touch of irony, Paul challenges the Galatians: *"Tell me, ... are you not aware of what the law says?"* (4:21, NIV). He seems to suggest that they should listen carefully to him so they understand the complete truth of the Law, something they might not get from the Judaizers. Paul makes an allegory from the account of Abraham's two sons, Ishmael and Isaac. Ishmael is the son of Abraham's union with Hagar, Sarah's maid. Isaac is the child born to Abraham and Sarah as a result of God's promise. Paul's audience would be familiar with this account.

Paul is drawing a lesson of faith from history. When the promise of an heir did not appear likely to be fulfilled, Sarah suggested that her husband father children by a slave woman. From the perspective of custom, Sarah's plan was acceptable. From the perspective of faith, it was evidence of impatience with God's timetable and lack of trust in God to keep His promise. Sarah was to be the mother of promise. But before that would happen, Hagar bore Ishmael. Several years later Sarah bore Isaac. Sarah and her son symbolize those who live by faith. In contrast, Hagar and her son represent the spiritually enslaved who live by Law. The child born to the slave woman was a son only in a physical sense, while the other was in the fullest sense born of the free woman, according to God's promise. Paul is saying that there are two branches of Abraham's family—one physical, the other spiritual. Those whose relationship to Abraham is only physical are in bondage; those whose relationship to him is spiritual are free.

Paul extends the analogy by connecting Mount Sinai and Jerusalem with Hagar. Sent away from Abraham's household, Hagar and Ishmael lived in the territory near Sinai, the place where the Law would be given. The line of descent of Christ was through Isaac, not Ishmael. *"Hagar ... corresponds to the present Jerusalem"* (Galatians 4:25); she is a symbol of the Jerusalem of Paul's day—the center of the Jewish religion, a place clinging to the covenant of Sinai and to works of the Law.

In contrast to Hagar, Sarah represents the heavenly Jerusalem, whose citizens are free in Christ. The Jews were familiar with the prophecy of a New Jerusalem, but here Paul is not talking about a future Jerusalem. *"The Jerusalem above"* (4:26) refers to a place that already exists in God's mind and purpose. The heavenly Jerusalem is the place where Christ reigns, and believers are citizens.

Paul reminds the Galatians of their place in a great family of freedom; they are children of the Jerusalem *"above,"* Abraham's spiritual descendants. Continuing the allegory, Paul refers to another incident concerning Isaac and Ishmael: When Abraham and Sarah held a feast to celebrate Isaac's weaning, Sarah observed the now 16- or 17-year-old Ishmael *"mocking"* (21:9), or teasing, her own young son. The unbearable situation came to a crisis, and Sarah asked Abraham to send Hagar and her son away.

The lesson Paul draws for the Galatians is that the Law and promise are incompatible; these two "sons" of religious observance cannot live together. As the slave-son could not allow the child of promise to develop in peace, so the Judaizers, Law-bound children of the Christian faith, cannot accept the Galatians' freedom. Recalling Sarah's words (Genesis 21:10), Paul instructs the Galatians to get rid of the Judaizers. Their legalistic observances cannot coexist with the freedom that comes to those who live by faith in Christ. Keeping the Law does not earn anyone a place in God's family.

Paul concludes his letter with affection, reminding the *"brothers"* (Galatians 4:31) that Christians are the true children of Abraham and of God. The way of faith can be chosen, but Paul warns that it is not enough to claim Abraham as father. One must acknowledge one's mother as well.

Personalize this lesson.

Typically, when Christians hear the word "backsliding," we think of a believer who has returned to a life of immorality. Paul's letter to the Galatians reveals that he was concerned that these believers were starting to "backslide" not into immorality, but into self-sufficient legalism. In the Sarah and Hagar analogy, Paul does not focus on Abraham's sin of adultery with Hagar. Instead, he focuses on the sin of choosing self-sufficiency over faith in God's promise. We should not condone immorality, but neither should we condone self-sufficiency and self-righteousness. In jumping to judge a Christian caught in an immoral act, we may be falling into the sins of self-sufficiency and self-righteousness. No wonder Paul would later counsel in this letter, *"Brothers, if anyone is caught in any transgression, you who are spiritual should restore him in a spirit of gentleness. Keep watch on yourself, lest you too be tempted"* (6:1). Will you choose to trust God's promises, and to humbly encourage fellow believers who are struggling to do the same?

Lesson 5

The Spirit and the Flesh
Galatians 5

Memorize God's Word: Galatians 5:13.

❖ Galatians 5:1-6—Standing Firm in Freedom

1. Explain the meaning of Paul's statement in 5:1: *"For freedom Christ has set us free."* (See also Romans 8:1-4; 2 Corinthians 3:14-17.)

   _____

   _____

   _____

2. What command does Paul give in Galatians 5:1?

   _____

   _____

   _____

3. What is the *"yoke of slavery"* Paul refers to in 5:1?

   _____

   _____

4. What does John 8:31-32 tell us about how a person can live a life of freedom in Christ?

   _____

   _____

5. What are the consequences related to trusting the way of Law found in Galatians 5:2-4?

    _____

    _____

    _____

6. What is the significance of linking *faith* and *love* (5:6). (See also 1 John 4:19-21.)

    _____

    _____

❖ Galatians 5:7-15—Freedom Threatened

7. How does Paul use these illustrations to help the Galatians see the problem in allowing legalism into their midst (5:7-9)?

    a. runner _____

    _____

    b. yeast _____

    _____

8. What caution does 5:13 give about misusing Christian freedom?

    _____

    _____

9. In Galatians 5:14, Paul reiterates Jesus' teaching in Matthew 22:36-40. What do you think it means to *"love your neighbor"*?

    _____

    _____

    _____

10. Read Luke 10:25-37. Do you know a *"good Samaritan?"* Who?

    _____

    _____

    _____

❖ Galatians 5:16-21—The Believers' Conflicting Natures

11. Read 1 Peter 2:11-12 and Romans 7:21-8:1. Peter and Paul make it clear that believers still struggle with their sinful nature. How should we respond to fellow Christians who struggle?

    _____

    _____

    _____

12. What spiritual truth found in Romans 6:14 allows Paul to make the statement in Galatians 5:18?

    _____

    _____

13. Break down the list of sins into categories. For each of the categories, choose an act that reflects a desire to *"through love, serve one another"* (5:13) in place of the sin. The first one is done for you.

Scripture	Sinful Acts	Acts of Loving Service
Gal. 5:19	Sexual sins	Sexual faithfulness and purity
Gal. 5:20a		
Gal. 5:20b-21a		
Gal. 5:21b		

❖ Galatians 5:22-26—Fruit of the Spirit

14. Which spiritual *"fruit"* do you think the world wants to see more of in a Christian? Explain your answer.

    _____

    _____

    _____

15. According to 5:25 and Titus 2:11-15, how does a believer achieve spiritual maturity?

_____

_____

_____

_____

Apply what you have learned. As Christians, we face the choice of living according to our own natures or living by the Holy Spirit's nature. Paul states in Ephesians 4:22-24 that believers must *"put off your old self, which belongs to your former manner of life and is corrupt through deceitful desires, and ... be renewed in the spirit of your minds, and ... put on the new self, created after the likeness of God in true righteousness and holiness."* Our challenge is to keep walking by God's Spirit so that the new self, given to us by God, reflects a Christ-like character. When we allow our old self to regain control, we need to confess quickly and by faith ask God to take over again. He will, and in time we'll become more consistent in our walk with Him.

Lesson 5 Commentary

The Spirit and the Flesh
Galatians 5

Paul continues to address the spiritual children of the *"free woman"*
(4:31) and begins an appeal to reject the Judaizers' teaching. He urges
the Galatians to hold on to their freedom from the Law and its curse.
In a larger sense, freedom means deliverance from sin's guilt and power,
from God's wrath, and from Satan's power. So, Paul commands: *"Stand
firm"* (Galatians 5:1). Because of what God *has done*, believers must act.
Gentile Christians, who have been freed from pagan religions, should
not now submit to Judaism's bondage. Paul calls the Law's regulations
and manmade traditions *"a yoke of slavery"* (5:1).

Freedom Threatened by Legalism

The yoke Paul wants the Galatians to avoid is circumcision. Circumcision
is to the Law as a ring is to marriage: a pledge, a sign. The letter repeatedly
says that Christ has freed believers from the Law's demands. Circumcision
is not in itself an obstacle to salvation unless it is evidence of one's
dependence on the Law. If the Galatians revert to the single regulation of
circumcision, they bind themselves to keeping the whole Law.

The phrase, *"you have fallen away from grace"* (5:4) confronts the
Galatians with the consequences of choosing to be circumcised: they
are placing trust in something other than grace. Circumcision does not
matter. What matters is *"faith working through love"* (5:6).

A metaphor of a runner illustrates the problems the false teachers
are creating. Someone has interfered with the Galatians' race, forcing
them to break their pace or even become disqualified. Paul assures the
churches that the interference does not come from God—*"Him who
calls you"* (5:8).

Most likely, *"persuasion"* refers to the Judaizers' influences and pressures. Like the bad apple that affects the entire barrel, a little yeast penetrates the entire dough. For the church, a little error is dangerous and can make the difference between truth and heresy. The Judaizers are proud of their works and see Christ and His death on the cross as offensive.

Freedom in Love

Paul discusses the practical implications of Christian freedom. Christians should live free from undue restrictions and prohibitions, but, Paul warns, *"Do not use your freedom as an opportunity for the flesh"* (5:13). Freedom must be properly exercised or license will result. He uses two terms interchangeably—*the flesh and sinful nature*—to represent sinfulness characterized by lusts and passions. These terms refer to the weakness of human nature, not the physical body. This flesh, Paul states, is corrupted at its source.

The "slavery" the Galatians should freely indulge in is *"to serve one another"* (5:13). Paul wants them to escape the bondage of their sinful natures by becoming willing servants in mutual love. All the Law and the Prophets depend on these two commandments: loving God and loving one's neighbor. In contrast, Galatians 5:15 reveals a frightening picture: church members are depicted as rushing at each other like wild beasts. Lack of love produces attitudes and actions that will destroy their fellowship.

Freedom in Practice

Now Paul explores how God's Spirit, operating through faith and love, makes a life of service possible: *"Walk by the Spirit, and you will not gratify the desires of the flesh"* (Galatians 5:16). To *"walk by the Spirit"* is to lead a life governed by the Spirit's guidance and power. The verb used here speaks of habitual action—keep on walking. There is a fierce and unrelenting conflict between the flesh and Spirit to establish control over our wills. But Christians are not helpless against the sinful nature.

The Works of the Flesh

Paul lists some of the results of the power struggle between selfish, sinful impulses and the Spirit's influence. The first three are sexual sins: immorality (fornication, forbidden sexual relations), impurity (uncleanness, any kind of impurity in thought or practice), and debauchery (lasciviousness, flagrant public display of indecent behavior). The next two relate to religious practices: idolatry (worship of false gods) and witchcraft (sorcery, any kind of magic art). Paul's list of societal sins includes hatred, discord, jealousy, fits of rage, selfish ambition, dissension, factions, envy, drunkenness, and orgies.

The Fruit of the Spirit

In contrast, Paul describes the *"fruit of the Spirit"* (5:22); the singular *"fruit"* suggests unity. The Spirit produces Christ-like character in believers' attitudes and behavior. Paul then lists nine qualities of this fruit of the Spirit that should be increasingly evident in a believer's life. Legal restraints are unnecessary when these Christian virtues are evident: *"Those who belong to Christ Jesus have crucified the flesh with its passions and desires"* (5:24). Here, crucifixion speaks of an action; we have put to death the deeds of our sinful nature. We cannot do this ourselves, but God gives us a new life when we trust Christ's crucifixion for us. Through the Holy Spirit, we begin to reflect Christ's character.

Think about the less obvious sins Paul lists. The Galatians may not have been involved in sins of sexual immorality, but when Paul added *"enmity, strife, jealousy, fits of anger, rivalries, dissensions, divisions, envy"* (Galatians 5:20-21), he was pointing out that in God's eyes wrong thoughts and attitudes are as bad as sins of immorality. Yet we often tend to treat such sins as unavoidable. As we'll see in chapter 6, we need to *"restore* [one who has sinned, regardless of the type of sin] *in a spirit of gentleness."* As we do so, we *"fulfill the law of Christ."*

Walking in the Spirit

The apostle includes himself in the concluding exhortations. The first one—*"let us keep in step with the Spirit"* (Galatians 5:25)—means *to keep in line,* as in military formation or dancing. The second plea warns against feeling unduly important, combative, and jealous (5:26). These characteristics are part of our sinful nature, which still struggles to assert itself. Walking step by step, daily, in close fellowship with the Spirit offers the source of power to overcome. The greatest challenge to believers lies in the ongoing responsibility to *do* what God has commanded on the basis of what Jesus has *done* for us.

Personalize this lesson.

☑ Paul presents the perfect balance between God's grace toward us and our proper response: *"Since we live by the Spirit, let us keep in step with the Spirit"* (Galatians 5:25). Keeping in step with the Spirit is our responsibility, primarily through prayer. He steers us away from conceit and makes sure that we have only *healthy* competitive attitudes. He helps us when our old nature flares into activity and negative feelings appear. He gives us the will to turn our thoughts in another direction. Every act of willing obedience to the Spirit builds Christian character. The more we choose to walk in the Spirit the less power the old nature has so that we are daily becoming what God has declared us to be—His dear children, bearing His likeness.

Lesson 6

Love in Action
Galatians 6

Memorize God's Word: Galatians 5:22-23.

❖ Galatians 6:1-6—Christian Responsibility

1. From these passages, what are examples of qualities that should be evident in a *"spiritual"* (6:1) person?

    a. Ephesians 5:1-2 _____

    _____

    b. Ephesians 5:19-21 _____

    _____

    c. Colossians 3:16 _____

    _____

2. How is the word *restore* (Galatians 6:1) different from reprove or excuse?

    _____

    _____

    _____

3. What attitude and action should characterize the believer who is restoring a fellow believer who has fallen?

    _____

    _____

    _____

4. What cautions are given in 6:1-5?

   _____

   _____

5. According to 2 Corinthians 5:18-19, what ministry does every Christian have?

   _____

6. What do the following verses say about sharing *"good things"* with those who instruct believers?

   a. 1 Corinthians 9:9-14 _____

   _____

   b. 1 Thessalonians 5:12-13 _____

   _____

   c. Hebrews 13:16-18_____

   _____

❖ Galatians 6:7-10—Doing Good

7. What are the two "fields" in which behavior is "sown" (6:7-8)?

   _____

   _____

8. What harvest will each field produce?

   _____

   _____

9. What point is Paul making in 6:7-10?

   _____

   _____

10. What helps you keep going on days when you are *"weary of doing good"*?

    _____

    _____

11. Write, in your own words, the teachings on love that you glean from Galatians 6:10 and 1 John 3:14, 16-18.

_____

_____

❖ Galatians 6:11-15—Becoming a New Creation in Christ

12. What would motivate those who *"force"* inappropriate or unnecessary religious behavior (6:12)?

_____

_____

13. How does Paul sum up the performance of those who *force* such behavior (6:13)?

_____

_____

14. What lesson can today's believers learn from this?

_____

_____

15. From these passages, explain what it means to be *"a new creation"* (6:15):

 a. Colossians 3:9-14 _____

_____

 b. Ephesians 2:11-19 _____

_____

❖ Galatians 6:16-18—Marks of Mature Faith

16. From 2 Corinthians 11:23-33, what do you believe Paul's *"marks of Jesus"* (Galatians 6:17) to be?

_____

_____

17. In the conclusion of this letter, peace, mercy, and grace are offered to those who follow Christ. How have you experienced each of these spiritual blessings as a result of following Him?

    a. peace_____

        _____

    b. mercy_____

        _____

    c. grace_____

        _____

18. Do you know of a believer who has stood up for his or her faith and bears the scars, like Paul does? According to Hebrews 11:35-40, how does God view such a person?

    _____

    _____

Apply what you have learned. The letter closes with a smattering of advice, warnings, and frustrations taken from daily life. But Paul also offers encouragement, peace, mercy, and grace. As we reach out to God to receive these things, He freely gives them to us. In turn, we can share the gifts He has generously given us by helping others, encouraging a friend, or showing kindness. Will you make a practice of looking for opportunities to *"do good to everyone"* (Galatians 6:10)?

Love in Action
Galatians 6

Practical Living in the Spirit

The word *"if"* (6:1) provides a tactful start to this chapter. *"Brothers, if anyone is caught in any transgression."* Fellow Christians who are consistent in following the Holy Spirit's guidance should handle such situations. A spiritually mature believer should gently restore the one who has committed the offense. But Paul warns those who counsel a fallen believer to guard against temptation, such as feeling superior or judgmental.

The law of Christian love and understanding involved here is more demanding than any fixed moral code; it carries a divine quality: *"Bear one another's burdens, and so fulfill the law of Christ"* (6:2). The Greek noun for *burden* denotes a *crushing weight*—an overwhelming burden beyond one person's ability to carry. Burdens could be physical, spiritual, financial, etc.

The apostle reminds the Galatians not to think of themselves more highly than they ought to think. Spiritual pride and conceit will prevent them from bearing each other's burdens. Humbly realizing that we need support from other believers makes us willing to extend that help to others.

Galatians 6:3 warns against misplaced confidence. Paul is not saying that people should think of themselves as *"nothing,"* for self-contempt would demean the Creator and Giver of all good gifts. Each Christian has the responsibility to *"test his own work"* (6:4). Each person must shoulder life's basic tasks and responsibilities. The Greek word *phortion*, used here, means *"load"* (6:5), and refers more commonly to a light pack carried by a person or an animal. The context suggests that Christians should relieve each other of *excessive burdens*, but each person should expect to carry his own or her normal load of responsibilities.

Bible scholars offer varying interpretations of Paul's charge to share all good things with instructors. Some interpret the verse to mean money and goods—pupils should pay their teachers and congregations their pastors. Others view it as a call to share spiritual benefits. Through teaching God's Word, the teacher ministers to the needs of the pupil, who generously responds by sharing with the teacher and other believers.

Sowing and Reaping

Galatians 6:7 commands, *"Do not be deceived."* Anyone who thinks that yielding to temptation is without consequences should consider the power of the flesh and sin's deceitfulness. We cannot escape the effects of our sin even if no visible harm seems to come of it: *"Whatever one sows, that will he also reap."* If God does not immediately punish a sin, we should not assume He is indifferent. The sin-corrupted nature produces a harvest characterized by the sinful acts listed in chapter 5; it has no eternal value. In contrast, *"the one who sows to the Spirit"* (6:8) produces the virtues Paul lists. The final spiritual harvest is *"eternal life."* An individual's entire life represents a sowing time. The harvest will reflect the sowing. Persistent obedience eventually bears fruit. Paul urges the Galatians not to give up—not to grow weary or discouraged when they do not reap an immediate harvest.

Paul's Final Admonition

"See what large letters I am writing to you with my own hand!" (6:11). Some scholars believe the letter was recorded by an *amanuensis* (*secretary*) or, as in Paul's other dictated letters, he wrote only the concluding verses. Our Commentary writer supports three views that seem to be reasonable explanations: (1) Paul wrote the entire epistle himself because no amanuensis was available, and he wrote in a large script, which differs from the neat, space-saving script of a trained secretary; (2) he is emphasizing that the conclusion, obviously not dictated, conveys his sincerity and marks the dictated letter as genuine; (3) he wrote large for emphasis, much as a writer today might underline important thoughts.

Glorying in the Cross

Paul declares he will boast only *"in the cross of our Lord Jesus Christ"* (6:14). The cross was an object of shame and disgrace. With all its dreadful associations, the cross continued to be a stumbling block to the

Jews and foolishness to the Greeks. Paul explains that the world has lost its meaning and appeal. It is dead to him. He adds, *"and I to the world."*

Think about the cross. It was an ancient punishment reserved for the vilest criminals. The word was considered vulgar in polite Roman society. In our century the cross is a sacred symbol—an object of hope publicly displayed in churches and other places. Sometimes its familiarity has obscured its meaning or bred contempt. Some look at the cross with no sorrow and no gratitude that God gave His only Son to die for us. For Paul, the cross was not a symbol of shame; it meant love, freedom, and victory. May we, like Paul, cherish the cross, as the reality of God's love and Jesus' victory over sin.

A New Creation in Christ

Again, Paul states that external rites cannot produce salvation; he reminds the Galatians that what really matters is Christ's transforming work in the believer's life. *"New creation"* describes those whose lives are transformed by regeneration or spiritual rebirth—their thorough reconciliation to God and release from sin's bondage.

Paul reminds his readers that his Christian service has resulted in physical harm, and he feels this punishment is sufficient to validate his ministry and to end the opposition. Whether resulting from stoning or scourgings, the scars on Paul's body belong to Jesus.

The Galatian Message for Today

Paul would not accept a divided church. If the Judaizing Christians had won their point, the church would have splintered into factions holding different opinions about the Mosaic Law. However, Paul does not call for unity at any price. He states his case and proves the impossibility of justification except by God's grace. The mark of a Christian, then, is faith responding to Christ's justifying work on the Cross. On this, Christians must stand in unity. The essentials of faith must not be sacrificed on the altar of accord. The church today must stand firm on essential matters of faith, unified in the belief that we are justified by faith in Christ alone.

Personalize this lesson.

Jesus said, *"If the Son sets you free, you will be free indeed"* (John 8:36). Paul proclaims and defends our freedom in Christ. We will face obstacles to that freedom, but whatever is presented as an essential *addition* to faith in Christ must be resisted as a step back into bondage. Can you think of some legalistic restrictions you have placed on yourself (and perhaps on others) that this study has freed you from? Has this study given you new insights into the Holy Spirit's desire to change you from within? Have you invited the Holy Spirit to free you from self-imposed efforts at righteous living and to ripen the fruit (the godly qualities) He has given you? Review the list of motivations you made when you began this study.

Small Group Leader's Guide

While *Engaging God's Word* is great for personal study, it is generally even more effective and enjoyable when studied with others. Studying with others provides different perspectives and insights, care, prayer support, and fellowship that studying on your own does not. Depending on your personal circumstances, consider studying with your family or spouse, with a friend, in a Sunday school, with a small group at church, work, or in your neighborhood, or in a mentoring relationship.

In a traditional Community Bible Study class, your study would involve a proven four-step method: personal study, a small group discussion facilitated by a trained leader, a lecture covering the passage of Scripture, and a written commentary about the same passage. *Engaging God's Word* provides two of these four steps with the study questions and commentary. When you study with a group, you add another of these—the group discussion. And if you enjoy teaching, you could even provide a modified form of the fourth, the lecture, which in a small group setting might be better termed a wrap-up talk.

Here are some suggestions to help leaders facilitate a successful group study.

1. Decide how long you would like each group meeting to last. For a very basic study, without teaching, time for fellowship, or group prayer, plan on one hour. If you want to allow for fellowship before the meeting starts, add at least 15 minutes. If you plan to give a short teaching, add 15 or 20 minutes. If you also want time for group prayer, add another 10 or 15 minutes. Depending on the components you include for your group, each session will generally last between one and two hours.

2. Set a regular time and place to meet. Meeting in a church classroom or a conference room at work is fine. Meeting in a home is also a good option, and sometimes more relaxed and comfortable.

3. Publicize the study and/or personally invite people to join you.

4. Begin praying for those who have committed to come. Continue to pray for them individually throughout the course of the study.

5. Make sure everyone has his or her own book at least a week before you meet for the first time.

6. Encourage group members to read the first lesson and do the questions before they come to the group meeting.

7. Prepare your own lesson.

8. Prepare your wrap-up talk, if you plan to give one. Here is a simple process for developing a wrap-up talk:

    a. Divide the passage you are studying into two or three divisions. Jot down the verses for each division and describe the content of each with one complete sentence that answers the question, "What is the passage about?"

    b. Decide on the central idea of your wrap-up talk. The central idea is the life-changing principle found in the passage that you believe God wants to implant in the hearts and minds of your group. The central idea answers the question, "What does God want us to learn from this passage?"

    c. Provide one illustration that would make your central idea clear and meaningful to your group. This could be an illustration from your own life, or a story you've read or heard somewhere else.

    d. Suggest one application that would help your group put the central idea into practice.

    e. Choose an aim for your wrap-up talk. The aim answers the question, "What does God want us to do about it?" It encourages specific change in your group's lives, if they choose to respond to the central idea of the passage. Often it takes the form of a question you will ask your group: "Will you, will I choose to … ?"

9. Show up early to the study so you can arrange the room, set up the refreshments (if you are serving any), and welcome people as they arrive.

10. Whether your meeting includes a fellowship time or not, begin the discussion time promptly each week. People appreciate it when you respect their time. Transition into the discussion with prayer, inviting God to guide the discussion time and minister personally to each person present.

11. Model enthusiasm to the group. Let them know how excited you are about what you are learning—and your eagerness to hear what God is teaching them.

12. As you lead through the questions, encourage everyone to participate, but don't force anyone. If one or two people tend to dominate the discussion, encourage quieter ones to participate by saying something like, "Let's hear from someone who hasn't shared yet." Resist the urge to teach during discussion time. This time is for your group to share what they have been discovering.

13. Try to allow time after the questions have been discussed to talk about the "Apply what you have learned," "Think about" and "Personalize this lesson" sections. Encourage your group members in their efforts to partner with God in allowing Him to transform their lives.

14. Transition into the wrap-up talk, if you are doing one (see number 8).

15. Close in prayer. If you have structured your group to allow time for prayer, invite group members to pray for themselves and one another, especially focusing on the areas of growth they would like to see in their lives as a result of their study. If you have not allowed time for group prayer, you as leader can close this time.

16. Before your group finishes their final lesson, start praying and planning for what your next *Engaging God's Word* study will be.

About Community Bible Study

For almost 40 years Community Bible Study has taught the Word of God through in-depth, community-based Bible studies. With nearly 700 classes in the United States as well as classes in more than 70 countries, Community Bible Study purposes to be an "every-person's Bible study, available to all."

Classes for men, women, youth, children, and even babies, are all designed to make members feel loved, cared for, and accepted—regardless of age, ethnicity, socio-economic status, education, or church membership. Because Bible study is most effective in one's heart language, Community Bible Study curriculum has been translated into more than 50 languages.

Community Bible Study makes every effort to stand in the center of the mainstream of historic Christianity, concentrating on the essentials of the Christian faith rather than denominational distinctives. Community Bible Study respects different theological views, preferring to focus on helping people to know God through His Word, grow deeper in their relationships with Jesus, and be transformed into His likeness.

Community Bible Study's focus ... is to glorify God by providing in-depth Bible studies and curriculum in a Christ-centered, grace-filled, and philosophically safe environment.

Community Bible Study's passion ... is the transformation of individuals, families, communities, and generations through the power of God's Word, making disciples of the Lord Jesus Christ.

Community Bible Study's relationship with local churches ... is one of support and respect. Community Bible Study classes are composed of people from many different churches; they are designed to complement and not compete with the ministry of the local church. Recognizing that the Lord has chosen the local church as His primary channel of ministry, Community Bible Study encourages class members to belong to and actively support their local churches and to be servants and leaders in their congregations.

Do you want to experience lasting transformation in your life? Are you ready to go deeper in God's Word? There is probably a Community Bible Study near you! Find out by visiting www.findmyclass.org or scan the QR code on this page.

For more information:

Call   800-826-4181

Email   info@communitybiblestudy.org

Web   www.communitybiblestudy.org

Class   www.findmyclass.org

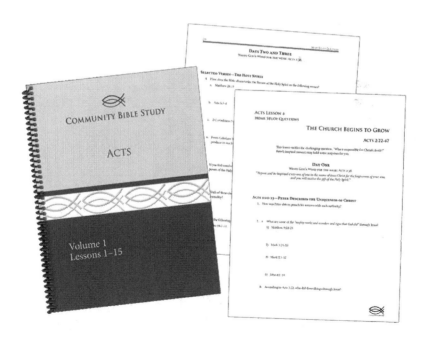

Where will your next Bible study adventure take you?

Engage Bible Studies help you discover the joy and the richness of God's Word and apply it to your life.

Check out these titles for your next adventure:

Engaging God's Word: Genesis

Engaging God's Word: Deuteronomy

Engaging God's Word: Joshua & Judges

Engaging God's Word: Ruth & Esther

Engaging God's Word: Daniel

Engaging God's Word: Job

Engaging God's Word: Mark

Engaging God's Word: Luke

Engaging God's Word: Acts

Engaging God's Word: Romans

Engaging God's Word: Ephesians

Engaging God's Word: Philippians

Engaging God's Word: Colossians

Engaging God's Word: 1 & 2 Thessalonians

Engaging God's Word: Hebrews

Engaging God's Word: James

Engaging God's Word: 1 & 2 Peter

Engaging God's Word: Revelation

Available at Amazon.com and in fine bookstores.

Visit engagebiblestudies.com

Made in the USA
Middletown, DE
28 May 2023

31627223R00035